MW01280306

MURR

The Bill of Rights

RIGHTS RETAINED
by the
PEOPLE

THE NINTH AMENDMENT

Hallie Murray

Enslow Publishing
101 W. 23rd Street
Suite 240
New York, NY 10011
USA

enslow.com

Published in 2018 by Enslow Publishing, LLC.
101 W. 23rd Street, Suite 240, New York, NY 10011

Library of Congress Cataloging-in-Publication Data
Names: Murray, Hallie, author.
Title: Rights retained by the people : the ninth amendment / Hallie Murray.
Description: New York, NY : Enslow Publishing, 2018. | Series: The Bill of Rights | Audience: Grades 5-8. | Includes bibliographical references and index.
Identifiers: LCCN 2017004987| ISBN 9780766085657 (library bound) | ISBN 9780766087439 (pbk.) | ISBN 9780766087446 (6 pack)
Subjects: LCSH: United States. Constitution. 9th Amendment | States' rights (American politics) | Exclusive and concurrent legislative powers—United States. | People (Constitutional law)—United States.
Classification: LCC KF4558 9th .M87 2017 | DDC 342.7308—dc23
LC record available at https://lccn.loc.gov/2017004987

Printed in China

To Our Readers: We have done our best to make sure all website addresses in this book were active and appropriate when we went to press. However, the author and the publisher have no control over and assume no liability for the material available on those websites or on any websites they may link to. Any comments or suggestions can be sent by e-mail to customerservice@enslow.com.

Portions of this book originally appeared in the book *The Ninth Amendment: Rights Retained by the People* by Kathy Furgang.

Photo Credits: Cover, p. 1 Chris Parypa/Shutterstock.com; cover, interior pages (background) A-R-T/Shutterstock.com; cover, interior pages (quill) Leporska Lyubov/Shutterstock.com; p. 5 Orhan Cam/Shutterstock.com; p. 8 Michael Ventura/Alamy Stock Photo; p. 10 Fotosearch/Archive Photos/Getty Images; pp. 12, 25, 29 Bettmann/Getty Images; p. 16 Jim West/Alamy Stock Photo; p. 18 ClassicStock/Alamy Stock Photo; p. 31 Saul Loeb/AFP/Getty Images; p. 36 Mladen Antonov/AFP/Getty Images; p. 38 Ethan Miller/Getty Images; p. 39 Joe Raedle/Getty Images.

Contents

INTRODUCTION

In 2013, lawmakers in Texas passed a bill that, among other things, had a number of parts related to access to abortions. An abortion is a medical procedure that ends a pregnancy. Abortions have existed for all of human history, but many people in America oppose the right to have an abortion for a variety of reasons. The Texas legislature wanted to limit access to abortions by requiring that all abortion clinics be linked with a hospital. They knew that this would cut down on the number of abortions performed, and many believed this was a good thing, even though it meant that women might have children they could not support or, perhaps even worse, that women might seek out less safe ways of ending a pregnancy.

The Texas legislature couldn't come right out and ban abortion, because having an abortion is a personal decision that a woman must make on her own. The government is not allowed to make laws that dictate the decisions people make about their personal lives or their bodies. This right is known as the right to privacy and is protected by the Ninth Amendment. People in the United States have the right to live private lives without government interference unless there exists some threat to community safety or well-being, and the right to privacy ensures this.

Yet when reading the text of the Ninth Amendment, one doesn't come across any references to privacy. In fact, the right to privacy is not specified anywhere in the entire Bill of Rights or any of the seventeen other amendments to the Constitution that were ratified in later years. That's because the Ninth Amendment is worded in such a way that it guarantees a range of citizen rights without having to specifically name each and every one of them. The text of the amendment states, "The enumeration in the Constitution, of certain rights, shall not be construed to deny or disparage others retained by the people."

The US Supreme Court building is located in Washington, DC, and is designed to look like classical architecture.

When the Bill of Rights was first drafted, it was feared that if each and every right of the individual was not clearly spelled out, people might be denied that right. Yet there are simply too many such rights to name. So, the catchall wording of the Ninth Amendment was designed to guarantee all individual rights are protected, even if they aren't explicitly listed in the Constitution. As a result, this amendment is one of the hardest to interpret and enforce. But over the years, the work of the Supreme Court has helped spell out and solidify some of these basic rights.

In 2015, health centers that provided abortions in Texas challenged the 2013 law in court. They said that abortions were actually a very safe procedure and that they should not have to be connected to a hospital to perform them. They claimed that the Texas government was not allowed to limit access to abortions because it wasn't actually an issue of community safety. In 2016, the Supreme Court heard the case and agreed with the health centers. It ruled that offering abortions was not a threat to anyone's safety and that by limiting access, the Texas legislature had infringed on women's right to privacy, their right to make decisions about their own bodies.

CHAPTER ONE

CREATING *the* BILL *of* RIGHTS

In the years that followed the American Revolution, the men charged with building a new American government faced an exciting yet challenging task. They wanted to create a government that would benefit every American citizen, one that wouldn't allow for the tyranny they had seen in England's eighteenth-century government. The US Constitution was written to spell out the fundamental principles that would govern the new nation. The first ten amendments to the Constitution are called the Bill of Rights.

The history of the Bill of Rights goes back as far as the history of the United States itself. After the conclusion of the Revolutionary War with Great Britain, the thirteen former colonies emerged as an independent nation. In 1783, the thirteen states completed the Articles of Confederation, which was a blueprint for how the federal and state governments would work. This document gave most of the new country's powers to

You can see a copy of the original Bill of Rights at the rotunda of the National Archives in Washington, DC.

the states, rather than the federal government.

The separation of state and federal powers was important to the newly founded nation. Americans were still haunted by the tyranny of the British government in the years leading up to the Revolution and wanted to prevent a similar abuse of power by a strong central government. But it soon became apparent that the federal government had too little power to be effective under the Articles of Confederation. For example, there was no executive or judicial branch of government (a president or Supreme Court). The federal government also had no power to collect taxes, regulate commerce between the states, or raise and fund an army.

In an attempt to strengthen the federal government, the states adopted the US Constitution in 1788. This provided the federal framework we know today, with an executive, legislative (Congress), and judicial branch. But the Constitution was not meant to stay the same forever. It is considered a living document, meaning it always has the potential to change. The changes that have taken place in the Constitution over the past three hundred years are embodied in its twenty-seven amendments, including the Bill of Rights.

FEDERALISTS AND ANTI-FEDERALISTS

Even before the Constitution was written, there was a lot of debate over what exactly it should say. The first American attempt at government was outlined under a set of documents called the Articles of Confederation. The Founding Fathers were wary of creating a government with a lot of centralized power, because they believed the centralized power of England's constitutional monarchy had led to corruption. In order to avoid this, the Articles of Confederation gave a lot more power to the states than to the federal government. It soon became clear, however, that if the United States were to stay united, they needed a different kind of government, with much more power given to a central, federal body. This realization led to the drafting of the Constitution.

The people who supported the Constitution and the new powers it gave to the federal government became known as Federalists. The people who opposed the federal government's increased role and influence—and therefore opposed much of the Constitution itself—became known as Anti-Federalists. The Federalists did not think that a detailed listing of the citizens' rights was necessary. They thought that if certain, specific rights were listed in the Constitution, then the rights that weren't listed in the Constitution might be threatened. The Anti-Federalists believed that if the people's rights were not spelled out, they would not be enforced.

George Washington presides over the 1787 Constitutional Convention, where the Constitution was signed.

George Mason, an Anti-Federalist from Virginia, refused to sign the Constitution because it did not include a "bill of rights" for the American people. Patrick Henry, also from Virginia, agreed. He argued that if the Constitution states that the people reserve their unalienable rights, then it must detail and list exactly what those rights are. There were many passionate debates over the subject, and both sides believed preserving citizens' rights was important—they just strongly disagreed on how best to do that. Finally, however, compromises were made, agreements were reached, and the document was signed on September 17, 1787.

DRAFTING THE BILL OF RIGHTS

Although Federalists and Anti-Federalists had compromised to create the Constitution, there was still a lot of discussion of the importance of listing citizens' rights. After the Constitution was ratified, Anti-Federalists got to work right away to raise the public's awareness that citizens' specific rights were not included in the document and therefore not guaranteed by law. This campaign worked. Only two years later, enough

AMENDING THE CONSTITUTION

Although it is possible to change the Constitution, it isn't easy. The possibility of amending the Constitution is detailed in Article V, which states that an amendment can be proposed by Congress if two-thirds of the House of Representatives and two-thirds of the Senate agree that it is necessary, or it may be proposed by a constitutional convention called for by two-thirds of all state legislatures. If this happens, the proposed amendment is sent to every state, where the state legislatures vote on whether to ratify, or approve, the amendment. If three-quarters of the states ratify a proposed amendment, it becomes part of the Constitution. It is really difficult to get that much approval to change the Constitution, because many people agree that the Constitution and its current twenty-seven amendments are enough. The most recent amendment is the Twenty-Seventh, which has to do with the salaries of people working in Congress. The Twenty-Seventh Amendment was first proposed in 1789 and finally became part of the Constitution in 1992, meaning it existed as a proposal for almost 203 years before being ratified.

public and political consensus had been built to introduce the ten amendments that became known as the Bill of Rights. These were ratified and went into effect in 1791.

Like the process of drafting the Constitution, the process of debating and drafting the Bill of Rights was

James Madison, the "Father of the Constitution," was also the fourth president of the United States.

long and difficult. Federalists and Anti-Federalists had fierce debates about what the rights should actually be and how the ten amendments should be worded. Many Federalists feared that listing the specific rights belonging to American citizens would mean that they were only entitled to those rights and no others. Basic and important rights long enjoyed by citizens might be lost simply because they had not been specifically mentioned in the Bill of Rights.

This is why the Ninth Amendment is so important. It put the minds of many skeptics at ease. The amendment specifically states that the rights mentioned in the other nine amendments are not the only rights to which Americans are entitled. Those liberties specifically mentioned in the Bill of Rights are referred to as enumerated, which means they're numbered, named, and specified. Yet, the Ninth Amendment defends individual rights that are unenumerated. These are rights that are not named or specified in the Constitution or the other amendments of the Bill of Rights.

THE RATIFICATION PROCESS

Even after the Bill of Rights was drafted, it took years to get the document ratified. Three-fourths of the states needed to sign the bill to make it part of the Constitution and make it the law of the land. It was not until 1791 that enough signatures were obtained to ratify the bill. Connecticut, Georgia, and Massachusetts never signed the Bill of Rights, but it was nevertheless passed by the other eleven states of the Union.

The process started with New Jersey signing the Bill of Rights on November 20, 1789. It finally ended on December 15, 1791, when Virginia provided the last needed signature to adopt the amendments into law. The chart below shows the dates that each state ratified the Bill of Rights.

STATE	DATE OF RATIFICATION
New Jersey	November 20, 1789
Maryland	December 19, 1789
North Carolina	December 22, 1789
South Carolina	January 19, 1790
New Hampshire	January 25, 1790
Delaware	January 28, 1790
New York	February 24, 1790
Pennsylvania	March 10, 1790
Rhode Island	June 7, 1790
Vermont	November 3, 1791
Virginia	December 15, 1791

CHAPTER TWO

EARLY EXAMPLES *of* "UNENUMERATED RIGHTS"

The Ninth Amendment is intentionally vague so that it can be interpreted as widely as possible. Yet this also makes it difficult for legislators, judges, and citizens to really understand what the Ninth Amendment means. The Ninth Amendment was not tested in court until over a hundred years after the ratification of the Bill of Rights, simply because many of the courts that were charged with deciding issues of people's rights did not think the amendment was strong enough to withstand scrutiny. Instead of using the Ninth Amendment, courts often looked at parts of the Fifth and Fourteenth Amendments that mentioned due process, or fair treatment under the law.

The role of the Supreme Court of the United States is to hear cases that involve federal laws like the Constitution and its amendments, and over time the decisions of the Supreme Court dictate how Americans interpret these important documents. Through the years, Supreme Court interpretations of the Fifth and Fourteenth Amendments have made these two amendments the main safeguards against the violation of citizens' rights. They ensure that citizens would be treated fairly and equally, without regard to wealth, status, gender, ethnicity, or race. Although the Ninth Amendment was created in order to broadly protect Americans' rights, it was often seen as too vague to provide any useful or meaningful guidelines for deciding whether an individual's constitutional rights had been violated.

ASHWANDER V. TENNESSEE VALLEY AUTHORITY (1936)

One of the first times the Supreme Court used the Ninth Amendment to help it decide a case centering upon people's rights was in 1936. *Ashwander v. Tennessee Valley Authority* didn't specify which rights the Ninth Amendment protected, but it did clarify the amendment to an extent. In this case, it was argued that the federal government overstepped its bounds in setting up the Tennessee Valley Authority (TVA). The TVA was developed as part of President Franklin D. Roosevelt's New Deal, a package of programs designed to end the Great Depression. The government took control of the valley's rivers, encompassing territory in Tennessee, Georgia, Alabama, Mississippi, Kentucky, North and South Carolina, Virginia, West Virginia, and Indiana.

The TVA began flood projects that would result in the generating of hydroelectric power. This would bring electricity, modern appliances and other conveniences, and economic development to a region long mired in poverty. However, the flooding prevented citizens from accessing areas they had long used for housing, farming, and hunting. The TVA also forbade private power companies from using

The Norris Dam and Reservoir is located on the Clinch River in Tennessee and operated by the Tennessee Valley Authority.

any of its electrical infrastructure or equipment. This prevented the power companies from competing for the right to provide electricity to valley residents and businesses.

The main question confronted by the Supreme Court in this case was whether the use of land by private individuals was a right guaranteed by the Constitution, even though it isn't stated directly. The Supreme Court's job was to decide if use of the Tennessee Valley was a citizen's right that could not be taken away by the government (even if that government was seizing the land in order to improve the lives and fortunes of those same citizens).

After hearing arguments from both sides and deliberating among themselves, the justices decided that the government could indeed use the land for the greater public good and that it had not abused its powers. The court explained that "the Ninth Amendment does not withdraw the rights that are expressly granted to the federal government." This means that the government's right to protect the public good—and the vulnerable people who make up the public—overrides any individual rights not expressly named in the Constitution.

THE HOUSING AND RENT ACT OF 1947

In 1948, the Ninth Amendment was again brought up in a Supreme Court case. A serious housing shortage developed in the aftermath of World War II. This shortage had two causes. The first was the large number of returning soldiers seeking places to live. The second was the supply shortage

A couple stands outside their new home in the suburbs in the 1940s. The number of people living in suburbs increased dramatically in the years after World War II.

created because so many materials had been devoted to the war effort and wartime industries.

There was a danger that citizens might be taken advantage of by property owners or landlords who might overcharge for properties during this period of high housing demand and short supply. To prevent this, Congress passed the Housing and Rent Act of 1947 to help regulate prices. Even though the war had ended, Congress was still enacting wartime laws to help the country recover from problems created during the armed conflict. But did this new housing law interfere with a property owner or landlord's right to charge what he or she thought was a fair price for a house or apartment? Was the right to charge what is deemed a fair price for goods or services a right guaranteed by the Constitution, even though this is not stated directly anywhere in it?

The Supreme Court decided again that the federal government did not overstep its bounds by enacting the Housing and Rent Act. It was agreed by the court that "war powers" included doing anything necessary "to remedy the evils which have arisen from [the war's] rise and progress." In this case, as well as in the case of the Tennessee Valley Authority, the efforts of the government to protect the interests of many citizens overrode the rights of the few individuals who might lose out because of the decision.

UNIONS AND POLITICAL PARTICIPATION IN 1947

In a 1947 case brought before the Supreme Court, federal workers who were members of a union called the United Public Workers of America argued that their rights as American citizens were being violated. A law had been passed about ten years earlier stating that public workers were not allowed to participate in political campaigns or engage in politics in any way because they were federal government employees. When they attempted to participate in political campaigns, one worker in particular was threatened with firing. Was the right to practice politics a right guaranteed by the Constitution, though one not named directly?

In arguments before the Supreme Court, the workers claimed that the Ninth Amendment guaranteed them the right to practice politics, but the justices did not agree. They decided that the workers could not violate the law simply because they felt there was a possible threat to their unnamed personal rights. The justices also said that any rights the workers had to practice politics would have been protected under the First Amendment, which guarantees freedom of speech, not the Ninth Amendment. Although these first few cases involving the Ninth Amendment did not help clarify exactly which unenumerated rights were granted to American citizens, some of the uncertainty would soon come to an end.

BREAKING UNFAIR LAWS TO CREATE NEW ONES

It is an interesting historical fact that some of the first Ninth Amendment cases that came before the Supreme Court involved people who, in order to claim their constitutional rights, actually broke the law. In the cases involving the Housing and Rent Act of 1947 and the United Public Workers, people chose to purposely break the law because they found it to be unfair.

In the case of the Housing and Rent Act, a landlord—the Cloyd W. Miller Company—purposely raised the price of its rents 40 percent immediately after the housing law was passed. The company did this to demonstrate that it thought the law was unfair. Cloyd Miller brought the case to court,

THE PATH TO BECOMING A JUDGE

A judge is the person who presides over a courtroom and decides on the consequences of a trial, often based on the verdict of a jury. Many cases are tried by federal circuit court judges. Judges usually start their careers as lawyers. They go to law school and after three years usually obtain a degree called a Juris Doctor, or J.D. They also have to pass a test called the bar exam, which tests students' knowledge and interpretation of the laws of the state in which they intend to practice. Each state has its own bar exam, because every state has its own set of laws. After working as a lawyer for a while, a person would either be appointed to a judgeship or he or she might run and be elected. The fact that many judges are elected forces them to do the best job they can and reduces the chances that they will issue unfair or incorrect decisions or become corrupt. The downside to elected judgeships, however, is that judges may rule based on perceived public opinion—what is popular—rather than by what the law requires. In some states, a committee appoints judges. State supreme court judges are appointed or elected depending on the rules of the individual state. US Supreme Court judges are known as justices, and they are appointed by the president to serve for life.

The Bill of Rights

which forced a series of judges to look carefully at the law and the issues at hand. Even though the Cloyd W. Miller Company did not win its case, it brought attention to the issue and forced the government to reassess its laws.

In the case of the United Public Workers, the people involved knew they were breaking the law by taking part in political campaigns. They chose to do so anyway, knowing the possible consequences—including job loss. They felt strongly that their basic rights as American citizens were being violated by the law. By telling their side of the story to the courts, they were able to force the Supreme Court to take a close look at the law and whether it infringed on people's constitutional rights. Neither the United Public Workers nor the Cloyd W. Miller Company won its case, but they did bring much-needed attention to the extent of the Ninth Amendment's power to provide unenumerated constitutional rights to American citizens.

CHAPTER THREE

The NEWLY ENUMERATED RIGHT *to* PRIVACY

The Ninth Amendment theoretically protects countless rights, but the vast number of unenumerated rights protected by the amendment also made it a weak argument in court. United States court cases kept attempting to identify a single unenumerated right that is guaranteed by the Ninth Amendment but not named elsewhere in the Constitution, and they failed to do so again and again. In general, judges did not consider the amendment to be a strong or practical protection of individual citizens' rights. Many judges and lawyers found the amendment more confusing than helpful. It was not until the Ninth Amendment became associated with a very specific right that it became used more often in the courtroom.

In 1965, the Supreme Court first heard a case that would be decided with the help of the Ninth Amendment and would identify an unenumerated right. This landmark case named the right to privacy as a fundamental, though unenumerated, right granted by the Constitution through the Ninth Amendment. The right to privacy could not be found anywhere else in the Constitution. There were provisions for protecting people whose privacy was violated directly by searches and espionage, but not for people who simply wanted to live their lives without interference, who wanted their privacy to be respected indirectly as well as directly. *Griswold v. Connecticut* was about standing up for the privacy of others and their personal lives.

THE RIGHT TO PRIVACY OF THE BODY

In the state of Connecticut, a law banning any form of contraception, or birth control, had been on the books since 1879. However, in 1961, Dr. C. Lee Buxton and Estelle Griswold, an executive director of a family planning center in Connecticut, handed out free contraceptives to their patients. They were hoping to educate them about birth control and help families prevent unwanted pregnancies. They handed out the contraceptives for ten days before being arrested and fined $100. Instead of simply accepting their fines, Griswold and Buxton fought the case and appealed the decision to a higher court. An appeal is a request for a higher court to reconsider the ruling of a lower court.

This appeal eventually resulted in the case being reviewed by the highest court in America, the Supreme Court. The justices considered the plaintiffs' argument that it was unconstitutional to interfere with the privacy of a marriage. The plaintiffs felt that it was the exclusive right of a married couple to decide that they wished to avoid pregnancy and choose the method by which they would do so. Griswold and Buxton insisted that family planning decisions were not up to the government and that the anticontraception laws currently in place were violating people's rights.

Dr. C. Lee Buxton (*center*) and Estelle Griswold (*right*) are shown here in the police station after being arrested for handing out contraceptives.

A majority of Supreme Court justices agreed that privacy was indeed an important right guaranteed to American citizens and decided in favor of Griswold and Buxton. The Supreme Court discussed in great detail whether this right should be granted under the Ninth Amendment or through other amendments. Ultimately, *Griswold v. Connecticut* was settled with the help of and reference to other amendments as well. Thanks to Judge Arthur Goldberg, however, the court decision was written specifically in order to help define the Ninth Amendment so that it would be useful in future cases.

The notion of privacy exists in some of the other constitutional amendments, but is not mentioned or named

DEFINING "FUNDAMENTAL"

Deciding what American citizens' fundamental rights are is no easy task. Even the Supreme Court has difficulty agreeing on what should be declared a fundamental and guaranteed— though unenumerated—right under the Ninth Amendment, and what should not be. Justice Arthur Goldberg, who helped decide the landmark privacy case of *Griswold v. Connecticut*, said that Supreme Court justices should look to the traditions and beliefs of all Americans in order to determine which ideas are the most fundamental. This method is good in theory, but it is almost impossible to agree on how to interpret the beliefs and ideas of every citizen, past and future. Another, perhaps easier way to determine whether a right is fundamental is to see if American lawmakers recognize the right. Do state laws allow or prohibit that particular right? How have lawmakers and judges in other countries viewed this supposed right? Ultimately, however, it is up to the justices of the Supreme Court to make the final decision as to what are a citizen's legal, fundamental, constitutionally protected rights.

The Bill of Rights

specifically. For example, the Third Amendment states that citizens are under no obligation to personally house American troops. The Fourth Amendment states that unreasonable searches and seizures of one's home and what is contained within it are not allowed. In large part, these amendments were added to the Constitution in order to better protect people's rights to privacy and private property.

In 1928, Supreme Court Justice Louis Brandeis wrote that privacy was one of the most fundamental rights protected by the Constitution. He and many other Americans agreed that the greatest protection provided by constitutionally guaranteed individual rights is the prevention of government interference in people's personal lives. The ruling in *Griswold v. Connecticut* ensured that the Ninth Amendment would become the key protection against government interference in citizens' lives.

ABORTION AND REPRODUCTIVE RIGHTS

After the ruling in *Griswold v. Connecticut*, the issue of reproductive and marriage rights continued to be debated in society and fought in court. One particular privacy issue centered upon the growing concern regarding a woman's right to make her own decisions regarding reproductive rights without government interference.

Abortion is the deliberate ending of a pregnancy. Abortion is by no means a new issue or practice. Women around the world had been getting abortions –both legal and illegal—for hundreds of years. In fact, the biggest controversy over abortion before the twentieth century was not so much the morality or legality of the practice but the safety of the procedure. Many women—as many as one out of three—died during or after the procedure because medical technology, knowledge, and expertise were not as advanced as they are today. In addition, many women were given crude surgeries in unsafe conditions.

The first state to pass a law banning abortions was Connecticut in 1821. The main intent of the law was to protect the mother's safety. Many other states followed suit. During the late 1800s, a movement began to ban abortions throughout the country. Some felt the procedure was unsafe for the mother and should therefore be outlawed. Others saw abortion as a moral issue and believed that the abortion of a fetus was the taking of a life, a form of murder. The Catholic Church was an especially influential voice in the growing antiabortion movement. By 1900, abortions were banned in nearly every state.

By the 1950s, medical practices had improved to the point that abortions provided by medical doctors were much safer for women. At the same time, the role of women in society and within the family began to change. Women began to have careers outside the home and wanted to have more control over their lives. As part of this development, the issue of reproductive rights became an increasingly important concern in the United States. And a person's right to privacy was at the forefront of the fight.

ROE V. WADE (1971–73)

By the late 1960s, abortion was still illegal in most states, including Texas. Two lawyers from Dallas named Linda Coffee and Sarah Weddington wanted to have the abortion laws overturned. To do so, they looked to Norma McCorvey. McCorvey had had a difficult life and found herself married and pregnant at the age of sixteen. She left her husband after he beat her. She had to leave her baby with her mother while she took a job with a traveling

Norma McCorvey was known by the pseudonym Jane Roe during the *Roe v. Wade* trial. Here she appears in her office in Dallas in 1985.

carnival. When she found herself pregnant again, she knew she could not support her new baby. Illegal abortions were unsafe in Texas, and she did not have the money to travel to another state for a safer one.

Weddington and Coffee thought McCorvey's story would help support their case for overturning the antiabortion laws when they presented it to the Texas courts. The issue of abortion had become quite controversial, and McCorvey's quickly became a high-profile case. To protect McCorvey's privacy, she was referred to as "Jane Roe" throughout the trial. The Dallas district attorney at the time was Henry Wade, and he was in charge of upholding the state's laws. So the case became known as *Roe v. Wade*.

The plaintiff's lawyers cited the earlier *Griswold v. Connecticut* Supreme Court decision in favor of privacy rights and reproductive freedom to bolster their case. They argued that Roe's right to privacy should be guaranteed by the Ninth Amendment. But this right had been violated because the government prevented her from making her own decisions about her pregnancy, body, and personal life. The district attorney argued that a fetus is an unborn person, and, therefore, an abortion would constitute murder. He reasoned that, even if someone had a constitutionally guaranteed right to privacy, that did not mean he or she had the right to commit murder.

The judges in the case sided with Jane Roe. They stated that "the Texas abortion laws must be declared unconstitutional because they deprive single women and married couples of their right, secured by the Ninth Amendment, to choose whether to have children." Even though the state law was declared unconstitutional, the judges refused to issue a legal order to prohibit it. So the case went to the Supreme Court in order for the state law to be repealed. In the meantime, abortion was still illegal in Texas even though the judges had declared the law unconstitutional.

ABORTION AND THE SUPREME COURT

As *Roe v. Wade* made its way to the Supreme Court, the issue of abortion became increasingly heated and controversial, and

Paul Ryan, a Republican congressman from Wisconsin and the Speaker of the House of Representatives, speaks to antiabortion activists outside the Supreme Court building in March 2016 following the case of *Whole Women's Health v. Hellerstadt*.

it remains so to this day. The Supreme Court justices heard the case beginning in late 1971. The case was re-presented in the fall of 1972 so that two newly appointed justices could hear all of the arguments from both sides. Finally, in January 1973, the court reached a decision. Justice Harry Blackmun wrote the court's opinion on the case. He wrote that "the Court has recognized that a right of personal privacy, or a guarantee of certain areas or zones of privacy, does exist under the Constitution . . . This right of privacy . . . is broad enough to encompass a woman's decision whether or not to terminate her pregnancy."

The issue of abortion is very complex, and the Supreme Court's ruling took this into account. The rights of the mother had to be weighed carefully with the rights of the unborn child. The court decided that as a pregnancy progresses and the fetus becomes more viable (more able to survive outside the womb), the fetus would have more rights and the mother's health would be more endangered by a late-term abortion. Therefore, the ruling specified that states could not restrict a woman's right to an abortion during the first trimester (months one through three) of pregnancy, except to demand that it be done by a certified doctor. In the second trimester (months four through six), states could only restrict abortions to protect the health of the mother. In the third trimester (months seven through nine), the state could interfere with a woman's access to an abortion in order to protect the rights of the unborn child.

REPRODUCTIVE RIGHTS TODAY

Since the *Roe v. Wade* ruling, abortion has become a fierce political, moral, and religious debate. The Supreme Court decision, far from settling the issue, seems to have fueled the debate, raised more legal questions, and hardened the battle lines. Many voters now demand that political candidates reveal their personal opinions on the issue because their legislative decisions will affect the laws of the state or country. The man or woman they vote for may someday be in a position to approve judges for state and federal courts—including the Supreme Court—who will sit in judgment of abortion challenges.

The case described in the introduction, *Whole Woman's Health v. Hellerstedt*, which also took place in Texas, is one of the most significant decisions regarding abortion that the Supreme Court has made in the past two decades. Thanks to the Ninth Amendment, the government is only meant to interfere in personal decisions like having an abortion if there is a threat to citizens' safety. As Justice Ruth Bader Ginsburg wrote in her concurring opinion of the case, modern abortions are so safe that Texas lawmakers cannot prevent women's access to them.

The abortion debate ultimately boils down to a question of individual beliefs, but it also gets to the very heart of questions surrounding Ninth Amendment privacy protections guaranteed to every American. To what extent can the government interfere in our personal lives and decisions? When does the public good or another individual's rights trump our own? In what instances does one individual's rights trump those of another individual, and why? What are the individual rights of parents, husbands, wives, children, and the unborn, and what happens when they clash? The Ninth Amendment has placed the issue of privacy and many other important individual rights questions at the forefront of our society's most impassioned debates and discussions.

CHAPTER FOUR

The NINTH AMENDMENT *in* CONTEMPORARY AMERICA

Ideas about the Ninth Amendment have changed significantly since it was first proposed. For a long time, it was more of a fail-safe measure to protect people from the government rather than a clear-cut defense of certain rights. The idea behind the amendment—the protection of people's rights that were not specified elsewhere in the Constitution—was important enough for the founders of our country to include it in the Bill of Rights. Yet the amendment was also vague and confusing enough that people didn't turn to it for support when attempting to defend and secure their rights in court.

Today, the Ninth Amendment is primarily associated with the right to privacy, or the right Americans have to live their lives with minimal government interference. Yet it is important to keep in mind that the Ninth Amendment is still vague, just as it was meant to be. It protects the right to privacy, but it also serves as a reminder to the government, judges, lawyers, and ordinary people that citizens have more rights than are spelled out in the Constitution. As a legal tool, it can help the courts to decide what rights should be protected by law.

Since the mid-twentieth century, the amendment has become more useful as an important way for people to win a guarantee of rights that they were often denied in the past. In some states, the right to privacy has been extended to cover many aspects of people's personal lives. These can range from the rights of gay and lesbian citizens to marry each other to the right of a terminally ill patient to die without extraordinary and invasive medical intervention.

THE RIGHTS OF THE LGBTQ+ COMMUNITY

If the Ninth Amendment guarantees Americans' right to privacy, why isn't gay marriage legal in every state? The case in favor of legalizing gay marriage nationwide can be made by arguing that the government is interfering with the privacy of marriage, just as it did in the case of *Griswold v. Connecticut*. The problem is that some people view homosexuality as a controversial issue, just as people view abortion and contraception as controversial. Some people feel that a romantic relationship should only be between a man and a woman, and that any relationship between people of the same sex is immoral and should be considered illegal.

Balloon letters spell "Love Wins" outside of a rainbow-lit White House following the 2015 legalization of same-sex marriage.

So who decides whether two people can get married? Is it up to the people involved, or is it up to the government that writes and enforces laws to create a fair and just society? This issue has long been debated, and it has generally been left to the individual states to decide whether to permit or forbid same-sex marriage. Lesbian, gay, bisexual, transgender, and queer (LGBTQ) people have gained a lot of ground in terms of overturning laws that discriminate against them, but marriage remained an elusive right. That is, it did until 2015.

In *Obergefell v. Hodges*, the Supreme Court ruled that all states must issue marriage licenses to same-sex couples and recognize any marriages legally performed in other states prior to the ruling. Although the Ninth Amendment was not explicitly mentioned in the argument, the decision to get married is one of many private, personal decisions that falls under the right to privacy guaranteed by the Ninth Amendment. The choice two people make to get married has no bearing on the health or well-being of people outside of that marriage, so the Supreme Court ruled that the government could no longer rule who could marry whom. There is a lot more to be done in terms of securing equal rights for LGBTQ+ individuals, but the battle for marriage has been won.

THE RIGHT TO INFORMATIONAL PRIVACY

Americans often feel they have a fundamental right to privacy. This includes the right to informational privacy. In the past few years, for example, laws have been overturned that demanded that employees give their private medical history to employers. These laws used to indirectly cause discrimination against employees who had an illness that necessitated time off for medical treatments or required a large amount of medical insurance payouts. People with certain conditions could lose their jobs or not be offered one in the first place.

These specific instances in which the laws that violated personal privacy were overturned are generally considered to be victories for fairness and justice. But what about situations in which the individual's right to privacy runs up against the general public's right to security? A person's

Body-scanning machines at airports allow Transportation Security Administration agents to scan a person's entire body for potential weapons.

right to privacy at an airport is becoming a growing concern and an international one as well. In an attempt to prevent terrorist acts, air travelers are being asked to reveal more of the contents of their luggage and carry-on bags. The kinds of items they can bring onto the plane are being restricted. Today, it is commonplace to walk through machines that can see if someone is hiding something under his or her clothing.

The right to informational privacy is becoming more important as people put an increasing amount of personal information on the internet. Our phones can track our locations constantly—should the government be able to use that tracking data in cases of national security? Should it be able to read private emails or track who calls whom in order to protect the people from potential threats? If someone does a web search for how to create a bomb, should the government investigate? Or is it an invasion of privacy to track web searches at all? Government policies must carefully balance a citizen's right to privacy with the safety of the community.

A protestor stands outside the Supreme Court hoping for a ruling on the 2005 right-to-die case of Terry Schiavo.

As our personal lives become increasingly reliant on the web, data about how we live becomes easier to collect. What to do with that data is the big question, both for the government and for everyday Americans.

THE RIGHT TO EDUCATION

Is the right to education a fundamental right guaranteed under the Ninth Amendment? In 1973, a Texas man named Demetrio Rodriguez was determined to find out. His children

ASSISTED SUICIDE: THE RIGHT TO DIE

Many believe that the right to die is a fundamental right that should be protected under the Ninth Amendment. When a person is terminally ill, should he or she be forced to accept medical treatment that would prolong his or her life, even if the quality of his or her life for these few extra hours, days, weeks, or months will be poor? Who should be permitted to decide that a person will not ever recover and should be allowed to die a natural death? Who should be able to decide when and how life should end? After much discussion over a number of cases, it has been decided by the Supreme Court that a person may choose to forego life-prolonging medical treatment. Yet it is still unclear whether a person may take actual steps to end his or her life. "Assisted suicide," where a doctor helps a terminally ill patient pass away peacefully, is highly controversial. Some people believe that if a natural death will mean a lot of suffering, then it is more compassionate to help someone die painlessly. Others believe that assisted suicide goes against the fundamental medical principle of the Hippocratic Oath, which states that doctors may first and foremost do no harm.

The Bill of Rights

attended a school in San Antonio that had little money. He felt that his children were not getting an education that was equal to that of the children who attended wealthier San Antonio schools. Rodriguez explained that the school itself was crumbling and that falling bricks would often disrupt classes and endanger the children. There were also discipline problems that the school was not equipped to deal with because the school had little funding for staffing. He pointed out that other districts spent over $200 more per student than his district did.

A lawyer interested in the issue of equal access to education took Rodriguez's argument to the Supreme Court. Together, they argued that education is a fundamental right of all citizens, and therefore educational opportunities should be equal for all children. That meant that every district must spend an equal amount of money on each student. The state of Texas fought against Rodriguez. It claimed that there was nothing in the US Constitution stating that everyone must have an equal education. It did not even state that education was a fundamental right. The state felt it was unfair to take money from wealthier districts and give it to poorer districts.

The Supreme Court voted five to four against Rodriguez. Even though the Supreme Court ruled against Rodriguez, he did not give up hope of obtaining an equal education for his children. He took his fight to the Texas Supreme Court to test whether the Texas state constitution guaranteed the right to an equal education for all students. A careful assessment of the case revealed that the state constitution does indeed consider education a right for all Texas citizens. The system of unequal school financing had to end. Since that ruling, other states such as New Jersey, California, and Kentucky have recognized that their state constitutions also guarantee equal education—and therefore equal funding—for all of their students.

CONCLUSION

There have been countless cases before the Supreme Court that brought up the question of rights that are not specifically granted by the Constitution. For example, should a woman have the right to nurse in public wherever she wants? Should people have the right to bring guide dogs in places where other animals are not allowed? Should handicapped people have the right to handicapped access to any building in America? Should a child have the right to sue his or her parents for child abuse? Should a child have the right to seek government protection from an unsafe home environment? Should every citizen have a right to a college education? Should all Americans have the right to live in a radiation-free environment? Should all people have the right to own whatever guns they choose? Should every citizen have the right to health care? Should citizens have the right to refuse health care if they wish?

These kinds of unanswered questions show the importance of Supreme Court decisions in our everyday lives. And they show just how difficult being a Supreme Court justice is. Weighing individual rights unspecified in the Constitution against those of the government, corporations, businesses, employers, and schools—not to mention against considerations of the public good—is an incredibly complex and difficult task. It requires a highly developed sense of fairness, balance, reasonableness, and respect for precedent.

The Ninth Amendment is no longer a "silent amendment," as it was for almost a hundred years after its ratification. It now shapes our daily lives and helps remind us that the rights stated in the Constitution are not the only rights we have.

THE BILL OF RIGHTS

First Amendment (proposed 1789; ratified 1791): Freedom of religion, speech, press, assembly, and petition

Second Amendment (proposed 1789; ratified 1791): Right to bear arms

Third Amendment (proposed 1789; ratified 1791): No quartering of soldiers in private houses in times of peace

Fourth Amendment (proposed 1789; ratified 1791): Interdiction of unreasonable search and seizure; requirement of search warrants

Fifth Amendment (proposed 1789; ratified 1791): Indictments; due process; self-incrimination; double jeopardy; eminent domain

Sixth Amendment (proposed 1789; ratified 1791): Right to a fair and speedy public trial; notice of accusations; confronting one's accuser; subpoenas; right to counsel

Seventh Amendment (proposed 1789; ratified 1791): Right to a trial by jury in civil cases

Eighth Amendment (proposed 1789; ratified 1791): No excessive bail and fines; no cruel or unusual punishment

Ninth Amendment (proposed 1789; ratified 1791): Protection of unenumerated rights (rights inferred from other legal rights but that are not themselves coded or enumerated in written constitution and laws)

Tenth Amendment (proposed 1789; ratified 1791): Limits the power of the federal government

Bibliography

Amar, Akhil Reed. *The Bill of Rights: Creation and Reconstruction.* New Haven, CT: Yale University Press, 2000.

De La Torre, Esther. "The Right to Assisted Suicide." Retrieved January 2017 (http://www.lonestar.edu/rightto-assist-suicide.htm).

De Vogue, Arianne, Tal Kopan, and Dan Berman. "Supreme Court Strikes Down Texas Abortion Access Law." Retrieved January 2017 (http://www.cnn.com/2016/06/27/politics/supreme-court-abortion-texas/).

Farber, Dan. *Retained by the People: The "Silent" Ninth Amendment and the Constitutional Rights Americans Don't Know They Have.* New York, NY: Basic Books, 2007.

Lash, Kurt T. *The Lost History of the Ninth Amendment.* New York, NY: Oxford University Press, 2009.

Levy, Leonard W. *Origins of the Bill of Rights.* New Haven, CT: Yale University Press, 2001.

Massey, Calvin. *Silent Rights: The Ninth Amendment and the Constitution's Unenumerated Rights.* Philadelphia, PA: Temple University Press, 1995.

National Archives. "Constitutional Amendment Process." Retrieved January 2017 (https://www.archives.gov/federal-register/constitution).

Oyez.com. "Whole Woman's Health v. Hellerstedt." Retrieved January 2017 (https://www.oyez.org/cases/2015/15-274).

Patterson, Bennett B. *The Forgotten Ninth Amendment: A Call for Legislative and Judicial Recognition of Rights Under Social Conditions Today*. Clark, NJ: Lawbook Exchange, Ltd., 2008.

Rehnquist, William H. *The Supreme Court*. New York, NY: Vintage, 2002.

Scalia, Antonin. *A Matter of Interpretation: Federal Courts and the Law*. Princeton, NJ: Princeton University Press, 1997.

Glossary

Anti-Federalists People who opposed the granting of increased power to the federal government and therefore also opposed the Constitution of 1787; members of a political movement in early America who wanted states to have more power than the federal government.

appeal A request for a higher court to reconsider the ruling of a lower court.

compromise To work together to find a solution that works for both parties.

due process Fair treatment under the law.

enumerated Named, numbered, and/or specified.

Federalists People who supported the new Constitution of 1787 and the power it gave to the federal government.

fundamental Forming a foundation or basis; basic; essential; most important; relating to a principle, theory, or law serving as a basis; an essential part.

interference Unwanted involvement in someone else's life or decision.

interpret To explain the meaning of; to make understandable; to bring out the meaning of; to give one's own conception of something.

precedent An earlier event, action, decision, or outcome that guides decisions in similar present and future situations.

ratify To confirm or approve something; to agree upon a proposed law and sign it.

tyranny An oppressive and unjust government; very cruel and unjust use of power or authority; harshness; severity.

unalienable Incapable of being transferred to someone else or taken away from the possessor.

unenumerated Not named, numbered, and/or specified.

Further Reading

BOOKS

Herda, D. J. *A Woman's Right to an Abortion:* Roe v. Wade *(Us Supreme Court Landmark Cases)*. New York, NY: Enslow, 2017.

Krull, Kathleen, and Anna DiVito. *A Kids' Guide to America's Bill of Rights.* Revised edition. New York, NY: HarperCollins, 2015.

Pohlen, Jerome. *Gay & Lesbian History for Kids: The Century-Long Struggle for LGBT Rights.* Chicago, IL: Chicago Review Press, 2015.

WEBSITES

American Civil Liberties Union (ACLU)
www.aclu.org

The ACLU views itself as the nation's guardian of liberty, working daily in courts, legislatures, and communities to defend and preserve the individual rights and liberties that are guaranteed every American citizen, including the right to privacy.

National Archives and Records Administration
(NARA)
www.archives.gov

The NARA is the nation's record keeper. The archives house the Declaration of Independence, the Articles of Confederation, the Constitution, the Bill of Rights, and the Emancipation Proclamation, along with other documents of national importance.

National Constitution Center
constitutioncenter.org

The National Constitution Center was established by Congress to "disseminate information about the United States Constitution on a non-partisan basis in order to increase the awareness and understanding of the Constitution among the American people."

Index